INVESTING:
MAKING YOUR MONEY
WORK FOR YOU

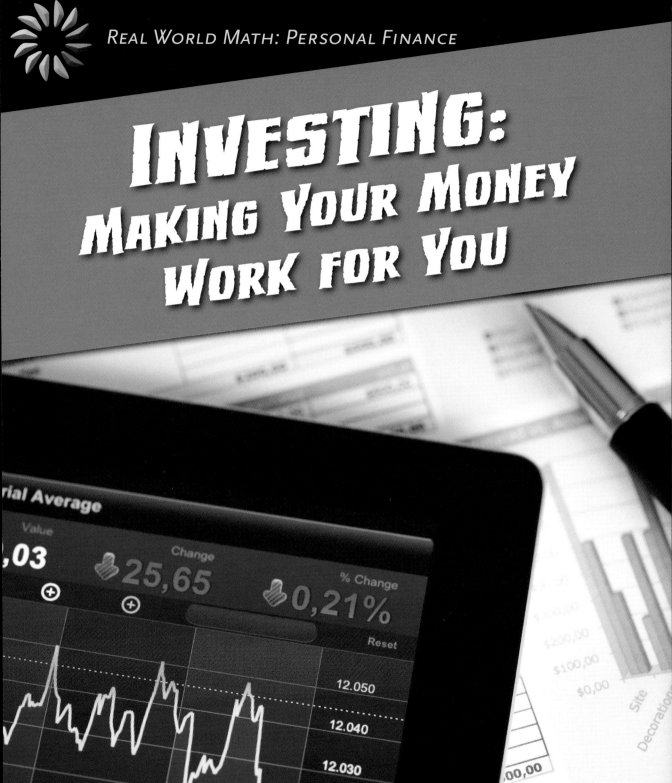

Peachtree

KATIE MARSICO

Published in the United States of America by Cherry Lake Publishing
Ann Arbor, Michigan
www.cherrylakepublishing.com

Math Education: Dr. Timothy Whiteford, Associate Professor of Education at St. Michael's College
Financial Adviser: Kenneth Klooster, financial adviser at Edward Jones Investments
Reading Adviser: Marla Conn, ReadAbility, Inc.

Photo Credits: © MicroWorks/Shutterstock Images, cover, 1, 21; © Baloncici/Shutterstock Images, 5; © Purestock/
Thinkstock Images, 7; © larryhw/Thinkstock Images, 9; © Goodluz/Shutterstock Images, 11; © larry1235/Shutterstock
Images, 12; © antoniodiaz/Shutterstock Imagse, 15; © Fuse/Thinkstock Images, 16; © JohnKwan/Shutterstock Images,
19, 27; © morrison77/Shutterstock Images, 22; © Rawpixel/Shutterstock Images, 25; © Volt Collection/Shutterstock
Images, 28

Library of Congress Cataloging-in-Publication Data

Marsico, Katie, 1980-
    Investing : making your money work for you / Katie Marsico.
    pages cm. — (Real world math: personal finance)
    Includes bibliographical references and index.
    ISBN 978-1-63362-571-6 (hardcover) — ISBN 978-1-63362-751-2 (pdf) —
    ISBN 978-1-63362-661-4 (pbk.) — ISBN 978-1-63362-841-0 (ebook)
    1. Investments—Juvenile literature. 2. Finance, Personal—Juvenile literature. 3. Mathematics—
Juvenile literature. I. Title.

    HG4521.M328 2016
    332.6—dc23   2015008971

Cherry Lake Publishing would like to acknowledge the work of
the Partnership for 21st Century Skills. Please visit www.p21.org
for more information.

Printed in the United States of America
Corporate Graphics

ABOUT THE AUTHOR

Katie Marsico is the author of more than 200 children's books. She lives in a suburb of Chicago,
Illinois, with her husband and children.

TABLE OF CONTENTS

GET IT TO GROW!

Have you heard the expression "Money doesn't grow on trees"? Maybe you heard it the last time you asked your parents for money! Well, it's true that money doesn't grow on trees. But it's still possible to make money grow by investing it wisely. Investing involves spending or setting aside money with the goal of ultimately making more.

Inflation, or an increase in prices, is one reason that investing money is often a wise choice. Years ago, farmers brought vegetables to town and city markets in horse-drawn wagons. Back then, vegetables cost pennies.

4

The price of vegetables has been rising over time.

Most vegetables today are still sold in markets in towns and cities. Farmers are still paid, but so are the people who own the markets. Shipping, storage, and other expenses also raise the cost of vegetables. Even though vegetables haven't changed much, they're hundreds of times more expensive than they used to be.

Setting financial goals helps people continue to pay for their living expenses even when inflation occurs. Financial goals are plans for the future. There are two types of financial goals—short-term goals and long-term goals.

You make short-term goals to pay for things in the immediate future. Examples of short-term financial goals include setting aside money for a movie ticket, a special book, or a birthday present. You make long-term goals to pay for more expensive things much later on. Long-term financial goals include setting aside money for a new bike or new computer, or even college tuition or to start a business.

Several different investment opportunities exist to help people accomplish their financial goals. Let's see which one works best for you!

LIFE AND CAREER SKILLS

Practicing good financial habits now will help you in the future. For starters, try to save at least 10 percent of your allowance, paychecks, and any money you receive as a gift. If possible, try to invest another 10 percent. Are you able to think of a few more financial habits you should work on developing now?

Before you go to a movie, you need to make sure you have enough money to pay for a ticket.

CHAPTER 2

SAVINGS OPTIONS

The best way to have money for the future is to make and save money today. Savings accounts, certificates of deposit (CDs), and government bonds are three different ways to set aside and also earn money.

Let's say you put your money in a savings account in a bank. With a savings account, you are able to withdraw, or take out, your money at any time. Because of this, savings accounts are often useful if you are working toward short-term financial goals.

In order to keep your savings account, the bank pays

you money called **interest**. Interest is usually calculated as a percentage of the money you deposit, or put into the bank. Banks typically offer low interest rates on savings accounts.

The higher the amount of money in your savings account, the more interest you will earn.

LIFE AND CAREER SKILLS

So, what do banks get out of taking care of your money? They use the funds you deposit to loan money to other people. Banks often charge a high interest rate on these loans. Meanwhile, they pay a low interest rate on savings accounts and CDs. The difference between these two amounts is part of the profit banks make.

You're more likely to get a higher interest rate if you buy a CD. This is because the bank is guaranteeing your money for a set period. When you purchase a CD, you agree to put your money in a special kind of bank account for a certain amount of time. This period generally lasts anywhere from one month to 10 years. At the end of whatever period you've agreed to, you're able to withdraw the money you deposited. (CDs are sold in fixed amounts, such as $500 or $1,000.) You're also able to withdraw whatever interest you've earned. If you withdraw your money early, however, you're charged a **penalty**. Usually, the penalty is that you lose a portion of your interest.

When people make big purchases, such as new cars, they often will need to take out loans.

Government bonds are one form of investment.

Government bonds also involve you investing your money for a set length of time. When you purchase government bonds, you are loaning the government money. In return, the government agrees to pay you an interest rate called a **dividend** yield.

There are different types of government bonds. People tend to be most familiar with I bonds and EE bonds. For both, there's a penalty for cashing in a bond that's less than five years old. The penalty is usually the loss of any interest earned in the last three months.

Whether you invest in a savings account, CD, or government bond, there's almost no chance you'll lose money. Though the interest rate is usually not high, you'll know from the start exactly how much you'll earn. Different types of investments offer higher interest rates but also carry greater risks. Keep reading to learn more about the advantages and disadvantages of these other investment opportunities.

REAL WORLD MATH CHALLENGE

Catherine's grandparents purchase 3 CDs for her. The price of each one is $2,000. Catherine knows that she must keep money in the CDs for 1 year. During that period, they'll earn 5.2 percent interest.

- How much interest will Catherine have earned at the end of the 1-year term?

(Turn to page 30 for the answers)

Do the Math: Money Market Accounts

For years, Samantha has saved money from tutoring and babysitting jobs. She's done the same with checks and cash she received as birthday and holiday gifts. So far, Samantha has saved $1,500.

She wants to buy a few items—including a new iPod and laptop—in the next year or so. In the meantime, she's hoping to earn as much interest as possible on her savings. Samantha isn't able to buy savings bonds because she's going to need the money in less than a year.

Tutoring is one way for people to earn money.

She doesn't want to put the money into CDs either. After all, Samantha doesn't know exactly when she'll find the iPod and computer she's looking for. Since she's not sure when she'll need to withdraw her money, she doesn't want it tied up in a CD. Samantha currently has the money in a savings account, but it's only earning 1 percent interest. Does she have any other options when it comes to investments?

Samantha's parents offer to help her put her savings into a money market account. A money market account

Most banks let you check your balance online.

is handled much like a savings account. But there are a few important differences between these investment programs. One is that money market accounts usually earn higher interest than savings accounts. On the other hand, money market accounts also tend to involve more restrictions.

For example, money market accounts typically require a minimum **balance**. This means you must keep a certain amount of money in the account. If you go below that balance, you will have to pay a penalty. And, with

21ST CENTURY CONTENT

In the 1930s, many banks went out of business. Thousands of people lost all of their money. The U.S. government formed the Federal Deposit Insurance Corporation (FDIC) to prevent this from recurring. The FDIC insures up to $250,000 in a person's bank account. So, even if the bank closes, you will always get at least part of your money back.

many money market accounts, you're often limited to a certain number of withdrawals per month.

Like savings accounts, money market accounts are a safe place to invest your money. But, while they usually pay a better interest rate than savings accounts, it's still not high. Are you looking for an investment that will help you earn even more money? In that case, you'll probably have to be willing to take a few more risks. Along the way, there's a possibility you'll lose some of your savings. Is such an investment worth the risk? Let's find out!

REAL WORLD MATH CHALLENGE

Frank wants to invest $1,400. Pick which of the three banking options below offers the most interest.

- Savings account: 3.6 percent annual interest on a minimum deposit of $1,000, and Frank invests his whole amount of $1,400
- CD: 5.1 percent interest on a one-year $1,000 CD, and the other $400 not invested anywhere
- Money market account: 4 percent annual interest (with a required minimum balance of $1,000 and no penalty on up to three withdrawals per year), and Frank invests his whole amount of $1,400

(Turn to page 30 for the answers)

Before you invest money, you need to know the risks.

stock

Invest ?

Cash

Bond

Do the Math: Stocks

Stocks are another type of investment. When you buy stock in a company, you are buying part of that company. You, the stockholder, share in the company's profits as well as its losses. You will make or lose money, depending on the company's success.

When companies earn a profit, stockholders receive payments called dividends. The more stock you own, the more money you'll earn from dividends. A second way stockholders make money is by selling a stock for a higher price than they originally paid for it. The value of a stock changes over time and is often affected by how the company is doing. Many people hold on to the same stock for decades. When they eventually sell it, it's possible that the stock will be worth 50 times more than what they paid for it!

The stock market is often unpredictable.

Getting involved in the stock market can be extremely stressful.

LIFE AND CAREER SKILLS

A stockbroker is someone who buys and sells stocks for others. Many people rely on stockbrokers to help them decide how to invest their money. Still, it is important to take responsibility for your own investments. Try to do some independent research to learn as much as possible about whatever companies you're investing in.

Investing in stocks has many other advantages, too. If you're a stockholder, you're able to be part of something you believe in or enjoy. For example, if you support environmental issues, you might be interested in investing in a company that researches new fuels.

But there are also disadvantages to investing in stocks. The biggest one, of course, is that it's possible you'll lose some or all of your money. The FDIC does not insure money invested in stocks. Another disadvantage is that if your money is tied up in stocks, you aren't able to immediately use it to pay for other things.

REAL WORLD MATH CHALLENGE

In January, Elena purchased 25 shares of her favorite video game company for $32.00 a share. At the end of six months, the stock went up to $46.00 a share.

- How much was Elena's investment worth in January?
- How much was her investment worth in July?
- By July, how much money had Elena gained?

(Turn to page 30 for the answers)

Investing in the stock market takes research and patience. It's important to read articles and listen to financial reports that provide information on how different companies are doing. Also, it's generally best to avoid trying to "time the market." Someone who times the market waits to buy a stock when the price is low in the hopes of selling it when the price rises. It sounds easy, but not many people are successful at earning money this way.

If you become a stockholder, you'll learn that taking a risk is sometimes part of making an investment. That's why you need to do your homework. Understanding all the facts in advance will help you decide if an investment is truly worth the risk!

Do your research before investing.

KEEPING YOUR BALANCE

At the moment, college probably seems a long way off, but you should still start saving money for tuition. Meanwhile, in the immediate future, you likely have other expenses such as buying your sister or brother a birthday present. Or maybe you want to go skiing with your friends this coming winter. Are you able to see why it's important to balance your long- and short-term financial plans?

Since these plans involve different financial goals, it doesn't always make sense to invest all your money the same way. This is why it often helps to **diversify** your

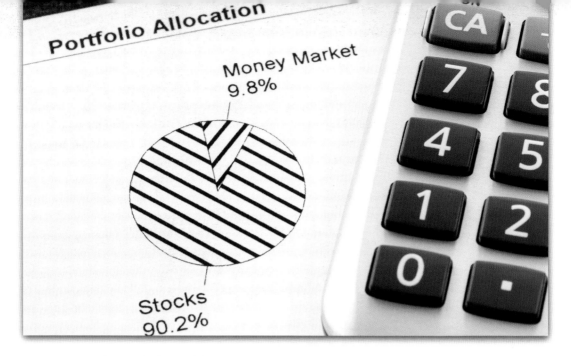

Portfolio Allocation

Money Market
9.8%

Stocks
90.2%

A diversified portfolio has money invested in more than one place.

portfolio. A portfolio is a collection of your investments. Having a diverse portfolio involves placing your money into different types of investment plans.

Maybe you'll decide to keep part of your money in a savings account. You probably won't earn much interest. But it will be easy to withdraw whatever funds you need to pay for purchases within the next year.

Maybe you'll also ask your parents to help you purchase some stocks. Of course, it will be harder to grab this money whenever you need it. But you'll hopefully earn

Once you invest in stocks, keep track of when their value goes up and down.

dividends over a long period of time. Once you're ready to head to college, these profits will certainly come in handy!

Diversifying your portfolio helps keep your investments safe. Imagine using all your money to buy stocks from just one company. What would happen if the company shut down? You'd lose everything! At the same time, think about the result of putting all your money into a savings account with a low interest rate. In 10 years, there's a chance you won't have earned much

[21ST CENTURY SKILLS LIBRARY]

more than you've deposited. With a diverse portfolio, you'll experience less financial loss and disappointment if one particular investment doesn't work out as planned.

No matter what type of investments you ultimately make, do your research. Talk to your parents and local bankers, financial planners, and stockbrokers. Ask questions, and check out the books and Web sites on page 31. Always remember that the more you save, the more you have to invest. And the more you invest, the more your money will earn money for you!

LIFE AND CAREER SKILLS

Before you start investing, get some hands-on practice! Begin by reviewing a financial report online or in the newspaper. Select two or three stocks to track for a month. Keep a chart that shows how their prices change. Review this information at the end of the month. Do any or all of the stocks still seem like good investments?

REAL WORLD MATH
CHALLENGE ANSWERS

CHAPTER TWO
Page 13
Catherine will have earned $312.00 in interest at the end of the one-year term.
$2,000 × 3 = $6,000
5.2% of $6,000 = 0.052 × $6,000 = $312.00

CHAPTER THREE
Page 18
The money market account offers the most interest.
Savings account: 3.6% of $1,400 = 0.036 × $1,400 = $50.40
CD: 5.1% of $1,000 = 0.051 × $1,000 = $51.00
Money market account: 4% of $1,400 = 0.04 × $1,400 = $56.00

CHAPTER FOUR
Page 23
Elena's investment was worth $800 in January.
25 shares × $32.00 = $800

Her investment was worth $1,150 in July.
25 shares × $46.00 = $1,150

By July, Elena had gained $350.
$1,150 − $800 = $350

FIND OUT MORE

BOOKS

Blobaum, Cindy, and Bryan Stone (illustrator). *Explore Money! With Twenty-Five Great Projects*. White River Junction, VT: Nomad Press, 2014.

Marsico, Katie. *Money Math*. Minneapolis: Lerner Publications, 2016.

Randolph, Ryan. *How to Save and Invest*. New York: PowerKids Press, 2013.

WEB SITES

Biz Kids—Saving & Investing
http://bizkids.com/themes/saving-investing
Watch videos that provide additional information on investments and financial planning.

TheMint—Investing
www.themint.org/kids/investing.html
Learn more about different ways to practice investing money.

GLOSSARY

balance (BAL-uhns) the amount of money in a bank account

diversify (dih-VUR-suh-fie) to place money in several different types of investments

dividend (DIV-ih-dend) money paid to shareholders out of a company's profits

inflation (in-FLAY-shuhn) a general price increase for goods and services

interest (IN-trist) the amount earned on money kept in a bank

penalty (PEN-uhl-tee) a fee charged when an agreement is broken

portfolio (port-FOH-lee-oh) a group of investments owned by one person

stocks (STAHKS) certificates that prove partial ownership in a company

INDEX